Verse

Birth, death, and the whole glorious mess in-between that we call life.

linda ruth brooks

Copyright © Linda Ruth Brooks 2018

All rights reserved. Without limiting the rights under copyright reserved above, no part of this work/publication may be reproduced, stored in or introduced into a retrieval system, or transmitted, in any form or by any means (electronic, mechanical, print, photocopying, recording or otherwise), without the prior written permission of the copyright owner.

ISBN: 978-0-6482985-1-9

Original artwork © Linda Ruth Brooks
Book design & creation: Linda Ruth Brooks
www.lindaruthbrooks.com

A copy of this book can be found in the National Library of Australia
Poetry/general

This book, and others by Linda Ruth Brooks, are available from: online retailers, bookstores and
http://www.amazon.com

Take down the love letters from the bookshelf,

the photographs, the desperate notes,

peel your own image from the mirror.

Sit. Feast on your life.

Love after Love, Derek Walcott

Contents

I'm glad I lived long enough 1
haiku 2
who's out there? who? 3
what hands are these? 4
Northern Territory 5
goodnight, my son 6
row 5 7
perplexed by sonnet 9
things I never told my sons 10
things my mother wished she'd told me earlier 11
she waits 12
side by side 13
my son 14
Australia 15
shoes 16
billabong 17
don't say goodbye! 18
(dec) 20
first cries 21
he thinks I sleep 22
I think he sleeps 24
I see ... your face 25
do you remember? 27
this 'growing old' thing 30
blessed be 31
behind whispering hands 32
computer woes 33
without voice 34
tsunami 36
The cat sat 38
waiting 39
doves fall 41
The heart remembers 42
gypsies and transients 43
Reasons to climb a tree 44

Reasons to climb a tree	45
your face	46
Birthstain	48
après…	51
tanka	52
rain	54
dance steps forgotten	55
shadows	56
weaver	57
to love	58
tears cannot silent be	60
leaves	61
that darkness	62
If you have the time	64
Clooney the Cat	67
I saw a homeless man tonight	68
I can't do that	69
breath of evening	70
he carried them home	72
I never dream	74
fear	75
light	76
hey mum!	78
chained	79
cancer	80
peace	81
poem to a child	82
dream holiday	84
icy voice	85
looking back	86
no longer	87
Letter to a child	88
A mother	89
I hope you don't mind	90
gone	92
indigo glass	93

chasm	94
silk	96
pedestal	97
automaton	98
ode to spring	99
flickering embers	100
Watagans	101
some people I know	102
into the light	104
I fought the Lord, and the Lord won	106
pity	108
gift	109
It's okay	110
meet me here	113
Silent witness to absence	114
unfaith-ful	115
She	116
The flies on your wall	117
Void	118
Teen wannabe queen	119
The idea of you	120
The portrait	121
Tears cannot silent be	122
without you	123
twice forever	124
Kitchen table	125
What was I thinking?	126
Author	130
Other titles by Linda	131

willows trail
tear-stranded chains
in mud-brown waters
at creek's elbow

we danced like water elves
singing summer's last song

billabong, linda ruth brooks

I'm glad I lived long enough

I'm glad I lived long enough
to stand beside you in the bakery and say
Don't even think about it!
I remember trying not to stare at the ice-cream display
and failing miserably.

I'm glad I lived long enough
to have to run around looking for *your* purse.
I remember I lost my purse so many times that you tied my money
in a handkerchief and pinned it to my dress with a safety pin.

I'm glad I lived long enough
for *you* to forget things.
I remember the words you said so often to me
'You would lose your head if it wasn't screwed on'.

I'm glad I live long enough
for me to bring *you* a salad roll for tea.
I can remember that you were 'cruel to be kind'
but could never let your children go to bed without tea.

I'm glad I lived long enough
to forgive and be forgiven.
I remember all the times you said 'Never let the sun
go down on your anger'.

I'm glad I lived long enough
to see the pride shining in your eyes
for all I have fought for and become.

But most of all I am glad I lived long enough
to love you, my mother, my friend.

haiku

summer fades...
cockspur coral buds
in deadwood

who's out there? who?

Who's out there?
Who? I mean who?

I
Who wanders and prowls on dark starry nights?
the nested birds have ceased their flight
vague sounds stir tense slumber
while I make lists for the plumber

Who scratches and taps with random beat
then taunts the night air before faint retreat
with frivolous regard for my weary plight
while I turn away from dawn's early light

Who flutters and flaps with keen disregard
is there a wild animal in my back yard
seeking to hunt, or just to perturb
rushing and bashing my sleep to disturb

Two cats are a courtin', (or something quite like it)
if they keep it up, I'll tell 'em to hike it
a tom plays the sax, another strums guitar
come morning, they'll bolt home with many a scar

II
Singing whales far away glide in the deep
furry creatures in forests scurry and creep
bats fly high, hang upside down
heedless of people, country or town

A slow drifting moon reigns in the sky
Southern Cross stars suspended up high
tall trees shudder, bend in pale moonlight
while I discern sombre songs of the night

what hands are these?

What hands are these
large boned, adept
patient hands

'C'mon mum
we'll finish it today
so you c'n use it'

C'mon mum
don't walk away
from a job half done
I'm here helping you,
y'know'

what words are these
deep timbre, intense

words that once were mine...

Thanks son
I love my light box
...and if I stood back
and let you finish and fix
my half-baked efforts
it amused me
to be you—
the boy you once were

Northern Territory

Never mind Jimmy Cook
Never mind all that fable
the Indonesians were first
to sit at our table

The Great Southern Land
neither conquered nor fought
but free trade arrangements
for trepang were sought

Never mind Alfie Deakin
Never Mind Georgie the Five
there in the vast north land
was an industry hive

Without cabinet ministers
writs or ICAC flaws
tens of thousands lived
within our fair shores

Never mind the Kimberly plan
Never mind the *un*promised land
exquisite beauty hidden
in timeless red-dust sand

Kakadu, Uluru, Kata Tjuta
what vision, what glory
in long-snaked river, in Arafura
and Arnhem land story

goodnight, my son

he slept in my arms
I was twenty three
my child, my son
five hours I cradled him
I didn't know why
I was just breathing him in
watching him sleep in my embrace

midnight passed
yet I stayed
all I knew was serenity
the bond of motherhood
all he knew was warmth
the familiarity of my heartbeat
from the time our pulse was one

one o'clock
time to say goodnight
I kissed his downy head
gentled him into his cradle
where his now sleeping brother
had once found slumber
had it been hours, or minutes?

morning crept in
I went to him
silently reposed
he hadn't moved
since my last lingering caress
he was gone from me
from this world, this life

I hadn't been saying goodnight -
I'd been saying goodbye

goodbye, my little one
I'll see you in that other morning

row 5

A contemporary haibun

At a funeral farewelling a friend of my parents, I was there as someone's daughter. I was reluctant to leave, wanting to be me - mother of a son long gone from life. I wanted to see his headstone. I didn't know why.

orderly rows bely
emotions' imprecise rhythm
searching for place

I'd vowed never go to go back after that one night spent in chilled agony where I lay 'til dawn. When tears were wrenched from some dark corner. Now, decades later, I couldn't find his resting place.

the funeral director
walked with me
to Row 5

We chatted as we wandered beside pristine rows of gleaming white, over lush green lawn. We grew up in this town, with the same school jokes, irony, small town secrets.

the plaque was grimy
my mother would've said
'it could do with a clean'

Past twin baby girls with bright porcelain cherubs on tiled perfection, together in death. Past the artist, the milkman, the newsagent, the dunny man, the professors, the wives and mothers. I knew too many of them.

shadows and light
sepulchered symmetry
ordered significance

perplexed by sonnet

Oh William, I thank thee for sonnets you gave
The beat, the pause, the lyric, the rhyme
I quite understand why they cause us to rave
each one constructed in a manner sublime.

My mother's pet phrases spring now to mind
Some repeated in halves; bare, incomplete
Although oft mangled they were one of a kind
Leaving the recipient muttering defeat

One of these gems was a glorified vow
(She had a manner of superlative speech)
T'was to eat her hat, a promise most hollow
For this undertaking was far beyond reach

If perchance I succeed to deliver a sonnet
I'll ponder if perhaps I should ingest my bonnet

things I never told my sons

I watched you sleep as a grown man
my heart melted as when you were a babe
I kissed your Size 10 toe
that peeped from under the doona

Photos of you are too numerous
for the walls of my house, now empty of you
but every smile, and every image
has instant recall in the memory bank of my mind

I kept your first Merit Award
I kept one of your odd socks
I kept the name badge from your first job
I keep you in my heart with every breath I take

There isn't a minute in my day
that I don't wonder if you're warm and dry
if you're hungry or tired
but mainly if you're happy.

I hope you remember me when ABBA
sings—'*Do you hear the drums, Fernando?*'
I hope you remember me
any old time at all.

things my mother wished she'd told me earlier

I didn't think much of myself growing up.

I didn't know my father well,
I wish I had.

I never realised how vulnerable I was until I gave birth.
I read all the books and thought
parenthood would be predictable, easy.
It wasn't.

I always thought you were beautiful,
even though you look like me.

Your father was my first love,
but I didn't think he had enough go in him.

I wanted to go to University but we didn't have enough money.

I fell in love with a reckless handsome man,
I thought he'd give me the world, he gave me pain—
I saw your father with new eyes.

I was afraid
to disappoint my mother.

Your father was my last love,
the best man I ever knew.
For the 30 years after he died, I couldn't call myself 'widow'.

I thought parents shouldn't admit mistakes.
I was wrong.

I never suffered fools.
Maybe I should've once in a while,
I can be a silly old thing myself.

Thank you.
I'm sorry.
It's all going to be okay

she waits

Ekphrasis on 'Evening' by Russell Drysdale

She waits

in evening's low glow

on brown ochre land

surrendered

to bare horizon's dim promise

I think I hear her story

while she waits

embracing

a single timber column

of her pale yellow house

I hear dreams washed by flood

heart cracked by drought

But these are mere musings

of my own faded story

perhaps...

she's only thinking

'Another five minutes

and I'll have a cuppa tea.'

side by side

Asleep together again;
at last.
They who hardly spent
a single night apart.
Fears, sorrows, joys;
forgotten.

Side by side
in peace
and serenity.
Their last thoughts
of each other—
and us.

Battles laid aside,
whether lost or won—
of little importance now.
Heartaches relinquished,
pride abandoned,
life's trophies jettisoned.

Side by side;
in peace
and serenity.
Their last thoughts
of each other—
and us.

Together again.
Through misty mornings
to extravagant sunsets.

my son

Contemporary ode

I knew him
before his eyes were stunned by light
his heart, so near to mine, pulsed in double-time
hummingbird in constant flight
a sign of things to come

and I
who feared altercation
trembled at such raucous ambition
demand and command—his first language
first vocal rendition

if I thought
I would seamlessly tame
this child of war, this wordy 'enfant terrible'
I soon learned my error

in still moments, cracked corners of peace
I pondered in transient tranquillity
When would this fracas cease?

one stormy night
as lightning flared and thunder roared
I sat outside myself and remembered
shadow people with tight words
taut smiles and frozen faces
retreating

so I celebrated him

Australia

Stretched summer days
chill of cool water
kissing sting of sun
rain on tin rooftops
trees shade saltwater lakes
midnight phosphorescence

timeless space, wind-carved ravine
red-orange, blue-purple
tulle fuchsia-skirted bottlebrush
orange-velvet kangaroo paw
wax flower, cowslip orchid
flame grevillea, hooded lily

horizon sharpened
interrupted by ocean
endless white sand
washed-pale cerulean skies
joyful splash of wattle
eucalypts crowd shorelines
towns crouch on coastlines

red-brick sliced mountain ranges
flaunting dark green treed cliffs,
amber-bright dawns
nullabor dreaming greets treeless horizon
red dust meets turquoise dessert sky
grey-green low succulents

salt-washed beach grasses
children slide on cardboard sleds
down terraced sand dune
Australia

shoes

(tales my mother told me)

shoes

thick card inserts

all the miles to school

poor protection from harsh winter chill

rough trail through scribbly gums

soles redone by father

frequently

billabong

willow's trail
summer rain adorns
tear-stranded chains
in mud-brown waters
at creek's elbow
where once we played
on bleached summer days
giggling and hiding
within playful strands.
moss-slimed roots jut
from clay-bedded banks
their velvety strength
forged there,
fixed, resolute.
How forgiving the branches
as we clung and swayed
how easily they bent low,
persuaded,
to join our play
as we danced like water elves
singing summer's last song.

don't say goodbye!

I'll miss you, you know, he says
I miss you every day, I say
It's not fair
Life's not fair
Sucks, he says

The dark shadows under his eyes
courtesy of some random gene
he gained through me
add poignancy to his face

The beach was great, wasn't it, he says
the surf tickled my toes, I say
I can't believe we found a puffer fish
No, that was a surprise
Random, he says

His eyes cloud again
I remember last night's conversation
he counted the number of times
he'll see me before I die
if he sees me twice a year

Why didn't you have me sooner? he says
I don't know what to say about that, I say
Yeah, I know, I'd be someone else
Kinda

Goodbye, I say
Don't say goodbye! he says
See ya later, then
Or sooner, he says, Please come ... and live

He turns and walks away
with that Stockdale gait he didn't have
before he became a working class man
I snap the image of his head and shoulders
then watch until the crowd swallows him

(dec)

two broken wounded kids
facing demons
I didn't know you, but I knew *that*
you didn't come softly into my life
you didn't leave gently

I wondered what I'd do
if I ever saw you again
I rehearsed random words
when stray thoughts flashed

with no rationale to care
I did without reason
your wounds cut deeper
on your way through my life. And
that makes you a part of me

who were you
neither of you added
or took away
so why do you feel part
of my losses?

then
on a page
two names randomly placed
incongruous, unexpected
haunting, wrenching

with the notation (dec)
rest in peace

first cries

first cries
break pale moon streaming
lungs raw at first contact
querulous crescendo
bereft of womb comfort
the die cast for
life

pale pre-dawn
struggling
into bright light
fresh hope

pink lips
seek tiny fists
blue eyes' myopic focus
finds mother, father
their hearts stretched
beyond understanding
as vulnerable in this moment
as their newborn child

he thinks I sleep

He thinks I sleep through his morning ruminations.
He doesn't know I measure his every sound my body straining.
The muffled moan, the leaden footfall,
the long shower, mist escaping under the door.
The opening and closing of the fridge,
the zipping of his school bag
He finds the note I wrote at 2 am
'have a good day, love Mum'.
He shuffles past my door.
I stay in my room not cocooned in sleep as he thinks.

My muscles battle to relax but I cannot rest, not yet.
I do not go to him.
If I do he will find it harder to face the day.
Harder to leave.
She is the mother, he thinks
I must tell her how hard all this is.
'I don't want to go, don't make me go'
'Let me stay here with you'
'You don't know what it is like for me there in that hell!'
'Now go, you will miss your bus.'

He will engage me in this daily battle;
this battle he must win.
He must face the world without me.
If I go out there to him I will hear of aches and fears,
injuries and bullies, boredom and dread.
I will murmur about responsibility,
of the future, of bravery and pride.
And then he will sigh, 'I do this for you, you know.'
'Do it for you,' I will say.
He will cut the last thread of connection and go.

But if I stay in here warm in my bed,
the sounds will be muffled,
his courage easier to find.
He will remember that he has to go.
I hear the low, slow burr of the sliding door open,
and then close.
I see him in my mind's eye
shoulders rounded by the cares of his world.
Old black hat jammed on his dark, curly head.
Hair the image of mine at his age.

The swing of the gate.
He has gone from me now
to fight the dragons in his kingdom one more time
To school; to try again.
'I'm trying so hard Mum,'
'I know.'
He's gone now.
My body slowly sighs
I sink into my marshmallow bed.
I drift; sleep finds me.

I think he sleeps

I think he sleeps through my morning ruminations
the dread in wide-eyed midnight hours
those hours   grey with dull apprehension
the muffled moans   the leaden footfall

I find his text message at 2am
'Come soon, we'll work it out together
Love Bronson'

I speak of aches and fears
of boredom and dread, of injuries and failure
he murmurs about the future
of bravery and pride

'you don't know how hard this is,' I say
'That's enough about that,' he says, 'You can do this'
'I'm trying hard, Bronson'
'I know, mum'

'I need to stand on my own   not be a burden,' I mutter
'I'll save the washing up for you,' he says
'Great, I'll hose it down in the front yard'
'Hey, Bella—Mum's gonna wash up in the front yard'
Bella laughs

I sigh
shrugging into the day ahead
stretching to find the courage
to fight the dragons in my kingdom
I hear the low, slow burr of the sliding door open
And then close
I hear the swing of the gate
I'm leaving

I'm going home

I see ... your face

I see your face as clearly today
as on that first day
when I strode into the crooked three-bed ward
of the nursing home
in my crisp white uniform
young and full of life

I expected dull eyes paled by defeat
quelled by the hand you'd been dealt
the handover report as bleak as any I'd heard
'clinically blind, profoundly deaf,
bedridden, underweight, voiceless'

I'd never seen a more beautiful smile
when I touched your face

you came to know me
in that brief season
when there was so little to know
no words to breach that weary gap
I longed for your story,
those things unnamed in Nursing Care Plans
while others railed and ranted
you turned soft kitten eyes
your soft hand found mine
your eyes closed in joy
how did you know me?

I know there's a heaven
for I've seen many hells
and in that place I will know you
perhaps you will be at Arrival Gate 52
or at the top of a spiral staircase to Cloud Nine
then we will run through meadows and mists
or whatever construct Paradise brings

do you remember?

(inspired by Ecclesiastes 12)

Do you remember
when we sat hand in hand
on that cusp
of eternity's dream
ethereal, found, complete
part of the vapour of heaven's kiss
knowing the time had come
to descend
to earthly place
for learning

To feel the sting of tears
the crack of heart
the break of soul
that would make us more
more than ever before
not to earn, but to become
our fingers entwined
knowing. But
not quite knowing
excited, seeking wholeness
wanting to know
but remembering
nothing could prepare us
for mortality
vulnerability, surrender

So here we are
mortal and defined
with edges and limitations
struggling and lost

wondering
if we found our earthly purpose
if we fulfilled
that divine vocation
that eternal becoming
knowing we would meet again. But
not knowing where or when

Did we remember
our greatest vows?
did we remember
to love ourselves
as heavens' blessed?
did we do that
and do it well?

And now we face
the edges crumbling
the evil days have come
the years draw near
those years of which we say
I have no pleasure in them

Now
Before the sun, the light
the moon, the stars
grow dark
before the clouds return
after the rain
the keepers of the house tremble
the strong men are bent
the grinders have ceased
because they are few
we gaze through dim windows

afraid of things on high
terrors in the path ahead
The almond tree blossoms
the grasshopper drags itself along
desire fails
mourners go about the street
the silver cord is snapped
the golden bowl is broken
the pitcher has been shattered
at the fountain
the dust returns to the earth
as it was

Do you remember?
do you remember
why?
do you remember
those last words
in the moment of our leaving
to this frail beginning
those words
whispered in heaven's sighs

remember
home

this 'growing old' thing

Saw an old woman today
sitting in her walking frame
curled intently
over her mobile phone
tapping away
happily

this growing old thing
is just going to keep happening
isn't it

crap
I don't remember
signing on for this

I arrived in this world
ignorant of it all
pink and wriggling
screaming and wrinkling
a portent...?

someone else signed me up
hey mum

never mind

blessed be

Blessed be the dream makers
the early morning bakers
the givers among the takers

Blessed by the truth sifters
the burden lifters
the sorrow shifters

Blessed be the rhythm groovers
the heavy-liftin' house removers
those every-day manoeuvres

Blessed be those who wait
those who silently anticipate
those who willingly participate

behind whispering hands

Behind whispering hands

lie seeds of suspicion

nurtured through the soil

of discontent

and spread

like midnight shrouds

unchecked

Behind whispering hands

in the womb

sheltered from the world

words begin in secret flutterings

draw tentative breath

and become

other

Behind whispering hands

lies become fact

twisting and turning

reaching beyond truth

grow, then fly

travel undeterred

afar

computer woes

Linda's computer was a rookie
it's systems were too slow
it followed every blasted cookie
and cost her lots of dough

Windows 7 came to save the day
but then the fonts just disappeared
Linda didn't 'laugh to see it play'
in fact, I think she jeered

Searching cyberspace for clues
brought random destinations
it fairly gave a girl the blues
to visit foreign cyber nations

A techo heard about her plight
and pitied her distress
he knew about fonts in flight
and decided to impress

With logmein one two three
a rescue was undertaken
there they were in old drive C
it couldn't be mistaken

without voice

A ghazal

The young soldier packs his knapsack, leaving her, without voice
To a country, to a war, to a people without voice

The dusty feet of refugee children kick a deflated ball
Solemn gazes through confining wire fences, without voice

Angel's feet dart in a destitute paradise, flighted but chained
Over landscapes torn, farmers blighted by drought, without voice

Ringing tones of confident corporations with swelling rhetoric
Boast promises they cannot keep, to laid-off workers, without voice

Strident arguments rise for sewerage to feed into pristine brooks
Developer's statements delivered by proxy, residents sigh, without voice

tsunami

Phuket, Boxing Day 2004

paradise
beautiful one day...
devastation
the next
walls of water
scrape the sky

    waves thunder
    tides plunder

voices scream
arms flail
reach and grasp
nature breaks open
a world upside down
lungs are bursting

    bodies tumble
    buildings crumble

idyll to hell
debris and chaos
tattered pages
names and images
pinned to endless boards
dead or alive?

    distance and despair
    in the fetid, dying air

minutes remaining on
battered mobile phones
thousands search
shelter with strangers
bloodstained torn clothes
donated by the destitute

    gratitude and grace
    one desire - a beloved's face

a family of five
tossed like matchsticks
and severed
two parents
three children
lost, then found

    sweet the reunion
    amid death and confusion

but we
in the blur
of everyday life
shiny new mobiles, but
odd little silences
pained separations

    hearts underground
    lost, not found

The cat sat

The cat sat
The cat sat on the mat

I CANT FIND MY LICENSE!
I don't want to talk about it
that's just silly, you say
I'm a woman
of course I want to talk about it!

I'm in South Australia
and I'm due for license renewal
my NEW SOUTH WALES license
that five year gold malarkey
usually a doddle ... but
I'm in SOUTH AUSTRALIA

New photo
Verification of identity mandated
(other than family)
Solicitor, counsellor, banker, teacher
Arrggh, don't know anyone who fits the bill—and
I CAN'T FIND MY LICENSE!

The cat smiled kindly
while I blithered blindly
sorting, collating, documentating
this form, that form—*irritating*

The cat winked benignly
while I fumed. Then finally
I moved the last thing in the place
(by now I was red in the face)

I shifted the cat

waiting

I wept
at the crossroads
the fork in the road

I will
not fight
to keep you near

I watched
as you left
with determined footfall
I wished
on evening stars
tiny specks, midnight velvet

I waited
for just a whisper
a tender, trembling word

I prayed
in guttural sounds
words lost their meaning

I trust
in memories faded;
in you

that
soul freeing enigma
called love

doves fall

doves fall
peace dies
brittle hearts
cold stone
buried guilt
false shame

muted innocence
muffled voice
cruel burden
harsh crime

soft tears
wrenched choice
crossed purposes
twisted lines
subtle whisper
sharp intent

listen now
light flickers
joy flutters
hope shines

divine comes

The heart remembers

Apology to the Stolen Generation—17 November 2009

The heart remembers what the mind forgets.
The heart remembers what the body lets slip into the past.
There is no sorrow deeper than the sorrow of unknowing
the sorrow of a truth denied.
While broad willows weep, we too lend our tears,
for those who travelled alone,
their childhood innocence stolen,
waiting for the heartache of generations
to be acknowledged, shared.
There are many to blame;
systems, departments, churches,
but ultimately people
their eyes closed, ears covered
to the voiceless,
abandoned, abused and forgotten.
It could have been us,
but it was you.
And it is you we will thank,
survivors all;
for finding courage,
for bringing outrage.
For hanging on, when the nation let go.
For speaking, when the world was silent.
We applaud you, celebrate and
remember you.

17 November, 2009: we witnessed history in Australia. An apology for the Forgotten Children. An apology that rose up on angel's wings, far above the lip service of politics, false charity and misdirected management. Many of us have our treasure boxes of photos and memorabilia. But, for The Forgotten, too often there are none. I am proud, humbled and inspired.

gypsies and transients

Gypsies and transients
come to my door

Sipping a little
a measure of life
accepting my company
bringing no strife

Leaning a little
giving a bit
then going back
to wherever they fit

Staying awhile
making it last
then moving on. Me
a thing of the past

I'm holding a memory
of being enough
on rare sunny days
when life had no rough

Techno is micro
connection is brief
life is staccato
congealing grief

Gypsies and transients
come to my door

Reasons to climb a tree

(age 8)

You (and the boy across the road) wonder what it's like to parachute with one of your mother's sheets 'borrowed' off the clothesline (she's at work).

You wonder what the world looks like from that high (you've seen skyscrapers on the new innovation called a television)

You wonder if the tallest tree in the street (conveniently next door) has the same view as the small ones.

You wonder how you can avoid trouble if the sheet tears on the downwards parachute journey

You wonder why adults say most of your ideas are half-baked

You wonder when they stopped having ideas

Reasons to climb a tree

(age 'over the hill and then some')

You wonder how many dead limbs need pruning

You wonder if you can reach them without having to borrow a ladder

You wonder if you'll get dizzy while you're up there

You wonder if you'll fall and get hurt

You wonder if you should have left the camera safely inside

You wonder how long it is since you climbed a tree

Then... you see the sun rising through the leaves

And... you remember a different kind of wonder

It's a beautiful world

your face

I touch the soft paper
of your face
gentling the imprint of age
my youth mirrored
in your searching eye
yellow-curded, near-blind
soft curved lips
you smile

    you love me

I touch the blue shadows
of your face
raw-lunged strain quiets
in our first embrace
fragile sigh
clenches my soul
breathing me in
you rest

    you love me

I touch the dark rasp
of your face
in roughness
find healing's soothe
your eyes speak
fierce low glowing
yearning breath shudders
you seek

    you love me

I touch the sticky flush
of your face
bright eyes
take first sight
fingers grasp
babe of my child
but strangely my own
you grip

      you love me

Birthstain

There's a silence that's darker than night.
There's a stain that will never wash out.
The valleys are scarred,
the hills are marred.

I am river, I am peace, I'm Australian
but my sense of place is uncertain.
The land of my birth is a mystery
there's a birthstain on my history.

Distant thunder prophesied war in Europe.
The Americas had fallen into themselves.
The Poles were currency for Hitler.
The Brits crossed the ocean
to the vast 'empty' space of *Australis*.
Pauper, priest, slave and king,
all ripe for a bout in the ring.

Chains on *The Charlotte* and *Friendship*–
an integral piece of my heritage
One ancestor purloined gloves and a shawl
for her sister to attend a child's party.
Another borrowed a coat slung loosely
at the door of a comfortable inn,
where the fire inside beckoned mutely.
One enterprising soul appropriated
fabric bolts and buckles
in astonishing quantities it's told.
The Old Bailey exposed their shame,
Newgate Prison bore their name.

I felt pride, they 'made good'
They were better than the warmongers
The weak politicians, the grasping profiteers
That was my song
But I was wrong

I'm a beggar, I'm a thief, I'm Australian
I'm ashamed of the carnage, the lies, the waste
That resides at the heart of my country's disgrace.
It was more honourable borrow a shawl,
to run off with a coat,
garner food, steal a goat.

My name is river, I am peace. But, now,
there's an indelible smear
on the word 'pioneer'.

après...

Hardy as a motivational speaker

Jane Eyre sets up a psychic centre

Hemingway preaches sobriety

Romeo becomes a paid escort

Rochester teaches anger management

Mrs Dalloway counsels for Lifeline

Byron as a hairdresser

Poe studies to be a mortician

Oliver Twist becomes a pudding magnate

Tolstoy takes up mime and flash fiction

Macbeth as a sales rep for hospital-grade cleansing agents

Sykes as a human rights lawyer

Mary Lennox starts a pesticide company

Mr Bennet cultivates a strain of tea with sedative effects

Kipling as an all-hours pharmacist

Richard III sets up a preschool and day care centre

tanka

how odd

surveying my potted plants

something's wrong

askew out of order

hurled on the roof and back ... by who...?

rain

Rain arrives sideways, on an erratic, busy wind. It's a wind with a deadline. It rushes through the gaps around the front door, as if it's been to many places and has many yet to visit.

In my last house the chill crept in with secret intent, seeped beyond yellowed gap filler – hardened from the scorch of sunny days. It brought a careful rain, slipping past new silicone barriers like water through teeth, leaving surprise puddles on large square tiles. And outside, its sneakier still – eroding the earth under the pavers, leaking into the underground ag-pipe canals, silting into the cavern of the stormwater drain at the front of the house.

The one that collapsed two years ago, taking torn shards of tarred road, like broken chocolate, but not taking my car. A neighbour, a real worry wart had told me not to park there – 'Your car will end up in China', she said. I shifted the car, just to keep her happy. Her hyper-vigilance amused me, and besides, she made a great coffee. When the road caved in we stood either side of the modest sink-hole and nodded wisely.

In this house the wind flies straight in, past the door – a fraction too small. It's a big blouse wind, a full frontal confident blast, no insidious gap-slipping manoeuvres, like a relative who's never been quelled, put in their place.

I'll fix you, I think. I buy rolls of 'superior quality gap seal (self-adhesive), and apply it to the door frame, not an undertaking for the faint of heart. The adhesive curls and unsticks at will.

It's done, a final slam. Bother, the bloody door won't close!

dance steps forgotten

'warm today'
she turns and smiles
soft words
simply spoken
but they bruise me
a bridge to a stranger
candidly offered
but they intrude
I murmur
something
nothing
eyes down

seeking to be as alone
on the outside
as the inside

the map has faded
even the new moon is jaded
the destination too far
where the fold lines lay
the compass lies broken
have all the words been spoken?

dance steps forgotten?

shadows

I have never chosen a dark alley.
Have never slipped joyfully through the velvet night.

I see shadows in daylight.
I see other's fierce embrace of the world and its wonder,
      and I fear.

For many years I didn't know its name.

Fear once was my companion.
My invisible friend.
The friend who warned me when danger was nigh
      as a child.

Looked out for me in a world everyone said was safe.
I did not know safe.

I did not know carefree,
      although my soul was stamped with joy.

Gentleness once brought me home to love.

For one short moment in time I was free.
There were no horrors in the shadows,
      day or night when he was near.

weaver

the heddle has fallen
the loom lays bare
yesterday's bright threads
strewn without care

no whirr of the shuttle
no more picking or shedding
no plain, twill or satin
no battening or beating

but here in the village
time has a different claim
the weaver's swift rhythm
is a mystic refrain

to love

The lights in the corridor were dim and low.
The evening shadows had lengthened.
A frail woman lies patiently.
She hears not.
She sees blurry visions of life.
I have come to check her.

It is we two alone in the dark night.
I caress her face gently
before switching on the light.
She knows my touch.

Her face glows with a joy
I've rarely seen in conquering heroes,
much less a bed-ridden tiny sparrow of a woman.

In all of what life throws me,
that look will always be
the measure of who I am.

She knew me.

tears cannot silent be

Goodbye
      my childhood hero
Live on
      sweet song of hope
God's breath
      is with you now
Soft and tender
      be the light
For your soul's
      heavenward flight

Today
      tears cannot silent be
      your struggling heart is free
Today
      you rest, safe at last
      earthly angst and pain is past
Today
      the aching void now ours to bear
      melding of sorrow the burden we share

Tomorrow
      when eternal day is dawning
      I'll see you on that other morning

leaves

Leaves
flutter and tumble,
then crunch underfoot,
from trees that have shed
their summer ballroom clothes,
sitting serenely in their dainty petticoats
of vermillion, sienna, ochre and gamboge.

Some
are ambiguous,
holding to verdant hues
that sit side by side with red,
orange, crimson, gold and aubergine
even the petite shrubs succumb to autumn;
soon the naked branches alone will reach elegantly.

Oh that we could die so beautifully,
to live again when spring whispers warmly.

that darkness
Robin McLaurin Williams (July 21, 1951 - August 11, 2014)

I didn't choose this
it came embedded
within the compendium of me
integral essence
of my totality
in my DNA
with my eye colour
my heart, my span
not part of any plan

Even as a child
it was there
often in the shadows
my invisible 'friend'
breezing a whisper here
twisting a lyric there

its language?
flinch of a tendon
trembling hand
morning angst
tightening heart
misty mind. For
there were no words

Its coming - and going
no beckoning of mine

ah, but when it was gone
my joy was pure
so pure, so high
it must have seemed too much
too exuberant, too playful
out of control

freedom was like that

But always
that bitter reunion
unexpected
urgent pawing at the door
each time more shocking
rending deeper
my bags of tricks to elude
sparser, weaker
more wearied
at its return

How raw I was then

without armour
naked, burned
aware of every single one
of humanity's sighs
each weary, leaden response
to my head-hanging depths
my spinning despair
as I fumbled at the solitary abyss
of that darkness

Remember only
that I struggled, and fought
remember only
how I loved, and dared
remember only
my laughter, my dreams
remember
the summits, the sunshine
remember
the best of me

If you have the time

I raced out all aflutter
random nerves on edge
stopped at petrol station
kissed a man I know
a tall and handsome dude
took off in a hurry
came home to find a note
(scrawled by said handsome dude)
'You didn't pay for the petrol, but
I told 'em you were sweet
could you go back in?'
      if you have the time

I had to be at a meeting
had to read a piece
see some friends and mingle
in a place I seldom fit, but
greeted with warmth and kindness
I guess I get things wrong
well, that's nothing new to you
you gave superior Chinese burns
then knocked anyone down
who laid a hand on me
I just wanted to tell you
      if you have the time

the hardest reading ever
kinda rare for me, but
something new to you
you've heard my every babbling
from the cradle through and through
I read a nursing story
a patient kind and pure

I dedicated the reading
to my childhood hero,
to my brother, to you
just thought I'd let you know
      if you have the time

and now
an angel has come whispering
with amber golden voice
to take you away forever
so few words remaining
so little left to say, but
I just wanted to ask you
when you glide on weightless wings
painfree and complete
could you drop by my place
drop a kiss upon my cheek?
      if you have the time

Clooney the Cat

Clooney the Cat
who knows where it's at
(*the food that is, and not much else*)

that fearless ginger who flinches at noise
but calmly sits to groom with great poise

who faces the outdoors with skittish elan
and acts like he's part of some marvellous plan

has today, yes today, at the ripe age of a quarter year
brought home his first kill, displaying no fear

that's odd, I thought, this kitty thinks I'm a mug
he's brought a torn corner of an old sheepskin rug

I saw a homeless man tonight

slender days
crisp and flinching
icy grass stalks snap
winter's midnight—5 pm
he's late unlike him

my son: he who wrenches me
from dreams of hazed confusion
to wake in disarray
come and spend, mum, spend *time*

he comes clumping inside
bringing shards of frozen wind
he paces, face bleached-cold
shoulders slumped

'I saw a homeless man tonight
it was pissing down rain
his beard soaked, miserable thing that
a wet beard, long too
he carried a bag, one bag for a life
what a country! I couldn't stop
the storm, the traffic—
he was gone when I went back
horrible, people without homes.'

those sac things ...? I murmur
leaning into his angst

yeah those, but ... hey,
I wanna take 50 bucks
to the homeless place

okay, let's go

I can't do that

You were
unprotected from my sorrow
unbidden
unbearable

I become enemy
detritus laid waste
I who shared your pain
as you shared mine

indefensible

amid the bounty
of gifts I bestowed
a broken hallelujah

you ask too much
...give up?

you taught me the song
its crescendos and falls
'I would do anything for love

but I can't do that'

breath of evening

evening breath

on my soul

touching

secret

depths of me

it's your birthday

do you remember...?

me

he carried them home

Just up the road lived my Uncle Gordon
an inspiration, a hero, a true gentleman.
His grey eyes twinkled with wit ever ready,
he was teased all his days for a pace that was steady.
Renowned for walking thousands of miles,
he welcomed all with the broadest of smiles.
In his opinion, all men were brothers,
in all that he did, he lived for others.

He was tireless, massive and strong,
a lion-hearted man who knew right from wrong.
Young men tested their strength on him,
but with his crushing handshake, he'd always win.
He wasn't a young man when he went to war,
it was then that his resilience came to the fore.
He didn't have pretension or worldly dash,
but he never did a single thing that was rash.

There were many people who set great store
in the honourable fact that he went off to war.
But for me as a child that mattered naught,
for the simplest of joys comprised the life he sought.
There were other talents, other things he knew,
along with the awesome strength of his sinew.
Things of spirit and heart, and a gentle kind of courage;
for he never succumbed to a moment of rage.

He followed, and fiercely believed in his country.
The eldest of eight, he was devoted to family.
And with all of his heart he believed in his God;
all these were the promptings for the road he trod.
Before he left home he worked with his father
carrying rail sleepers that were ever larger.
His spirit and soul were tried in the fire,
for he lived every day for a purpose that was higher.

Now God bless the men who carried a gun
but my uncle Gordon, he didn't want one.
Not *there* in the fields of destruction and death,
where many a soldier drew their last breath.
But from my point of view they were not any bolder,
for courage in hand, he stood shoulder to shoulder.
When bullets tore them open and they fell prone,
he nursed their wounds, and carried them home.

Now when he grew older, weary and sick
I grieved for his body, though his mind was still quick.
He leant on me then, such a gift of his choice.
One day he stumbled against me, and I heard a voice.
Now I'm not superstitious, or even crazy,
but what I heard that day will never be hazy.
A quiet kind of voice with a gentle tone
said, 'He's mine now. I'll carry him home.'

Gordon William Stockdale
Uncle, friend, compatriot

I never dream

I never dream, she said

I wish I didn't. I never stop dreaming, I said

*Well, I **hardly** ever dream...*

Hardly ever?

It's always the same one

Dreams are like that

I dream of my father

Your father?

I was only two when he died

Oh dear

I see his shadow in my dreams. I don't know how I know him, but I do. I couldn't possibly remember him. I was too young, she said

The heart is never too young to remember, I said

He seems to be far away–across a river. And yet so close.

I said nothing

I weep and ask to see his face. A voice says, 'not yet'

It took many years to dream of my father as whole not frail

Why does that happen? I'm 75. I'm too old for dreams, she said

Your hearts begs to differ, I said

fear

Hit me
and I will fear you

Hit me
and tell me you love me
and I will fear love

Never knowing if I deserve it
carrying a gnawing hunger
to possess it

Living in shadows
left with a void
I must fill
because you cannot

light
Inspired by 'Rainbow Trail' a painting by Greg Valeer

dim midnight hospital light
I think my waters have broken
the covers are thrown back
there's only crimson red
oh my god

                    filtered light
                    shining on
                    the secret trail
                    of my childhood
                    shadows cross the vale

fluorescent shatters
everything moves
too fast
the baby isn't moving
at all

                    the path shines
                    trees recede
                    their solid strength
                    enigmatic
                    in the dark background

theatre light blinds
gowned figures glide
swift and efficient
fighting for me
will my child live

                    subtle light
                    hues and tones emerge
                    shadows dim
                    angles soften
                    blending as one

soft dawn glow
my child lives
his raucous tone
a musical thread
of victory

hey mum!

Hey Mum
wanna spend?
music to my ears
wanna hear me bend?

harmonica, then guitar
blues and beat
effects and pedals
my Christmas treat

he bends the sound
as he bends my ear
isn't this great
it's been a good year

the boss gave presents
can you believe that
learning heaps at the new place
last one left me flat

here's a link
here's a song
especially for you
aren't y'glad I came along

you'll never quite know
the joy you bring
it's in the heart you open
the song you sing

yep, they're blessings
but in the end
your definition - the bounty
of the little word 'spend'

chained

short was his freedom
long was his chain
light at first
then heavy with strain

short his elation
long his despair
brief his enchantment
without a care

sweet the illusion
of leaving behind;
strong the delusion
peace his to find

sad the conclusion
to his swift farewell
leaving a master
with dread tales to tell

soft his return
harsh was the penalty
the chain confined him
ensuring captivity

bitter his repentance
silent his plea
slavery his lot
never to be free

haunting the music
lightly defined
the organ grinder's monkey
forever confined

cancer

close your eyes
it is not darkness you see

dotted like tiny stars
are the reflections of your thoughts

there's a glow in the centre

sometimes tinged with gold
sometimes silver or azure

feel your strength renewing
inner forces grow
each cell marshalling
stretching towards the light

hear the soft thud of your heart
as it sends healing to your soul
to every corner of the temple
of your body

you are healing
you are winning

peace

I fought pain
and I was trapped
I surrendered
and was free

I gave all
but I wasn't whole
I forgave you
and was complete

I wished you home
and you sailed further
I became home
and peace came

poem to a child

You are finite
you are flawed
you're not owed anything
life stings, growth is painful
a thorn keeps hurting
until you take it out
no wound heals
without time

Life gives you signs
sometimes you'll have to
Give Way, Stop, Look, Walk
watch for low bridges
you might have to pull your head in
a No Through Road is just that
One Way roads
won't always go your way.

'The Secret' of literal abundance
is capitalism in other clothes
better you have enough defeat
to make you humble
I wish for you—
speed humps to shake you
mistakes to break you
to make you the best you can be.

I wish you to know pain
so that all suffering mankind
will become your brothers
so your eyes will never turn away

I wish you to know joy
in the whispers of a lover
in the stillness of silent surrender to other
amid the noise of chaos.

As for me—
I'm not an ATM
I didn't get you at The Reject Shop
I am finite, I am flawed—I will stuff up
life will send you soft words
in lilting lyric and gossamer lies
know the truth
then live it.

dream holiday

a holiday, oh what a dream!
idyll rural diversion—(just feed the pets)
rippling brook, organic veg
a dainty cottage with modern conversion
seemed too good to be true
air fares paid, car and accommodation free

I knew how to respond

the website delighted with charming vistas
Oh dear, goodness me, there were sheep
I'd winded the last cranky ewe I encountered
it was butting the children, what else could I do?
Oh gosh, oh golly, there were horses too!
I'd been traumatised for life by equine adventures
winded by an ancient draft horse, no less
who stood where I was and not where I wasn't

I knew how to respond

photos arrived by email
the glory of the housing was for paying guests
the quaint servant's quarters had no heating
no cooling for hot Queensland nights
bathroom was 'just up the way'
Oh heavens to Betsy what could I say

I knew how to respond

icy voice

November rain
soft and warm
unlike September's
cold stings

a hope
a flickering candle
slow careful words
precisely placed

a trap
a poisoned chalice

November rain
soft and warm
birdsong celebrates
Heaven's tears of joy

words of ash
I am no one you know

looking back

she wore demure backless dresses
so he could drag hot kisses
down her spine.

throwing aside her inhibitions
she lay with him
romped   played
as they laughed like children
free of care in a way
neither had truly
been before.

of all the places
they went together
in that moment
each was the other's
destination.

for every
tearful farewell
there was a poignant reunion.
until the last time
when they clung together
like the lost children
they really were.

she lay beside
other men
to forget him
then she lay alone
to remember herself.

in her dreams when
time had no meaning
she saw only him.

no longer

I will no longer seek you
in the stilted corners of my heart
for I have not reached you
although my search was unyielding

I will no longer cast shadows
over your busy days
for I have not existed
in the realm of your desires

I will no longer follow
the footsteps of your days
for I have simply been living
in the land of my own dreams

I will no longer beseech you
in tentative apprehension
for your eyes are ever
scanning some other horizon

Letter to a child

I'm sorry you suffered
without voice   alone
the past is immutable
with its emotional distance
a price on affection.

It's not your fault.
you were a child
a child of the woman you became.

Now you reside in my grownup self
my precious inner child.
you are not alone or helpless
anymore, although you build walls
and towers to protect yourself.

I am your guardian now.
I have not done so well sometimes
the closer the connection
to others
the weaker my response
to protect you
I'm sorry.

I will do better
I am still afraid
but I will walk away
from those who isolate you
to take advantage
of your vulnerability.

I will take care of you
for you are me.

A mother

We stand together at the large window
        in the nursing home foyer.

Her frail hand raises in salute to the disappearing car.
        I see fear in her eyes.

Fear that she could love a son and lose him
        so often to an incomprehensible world,
                where her love has become desperate, clinging.

She loves with a hungry heart.

Slowly turning to me she says absently,
'The nurses told me I had cream,
        not milk when I fed him as a baby.
                He was such a skinny monkey.'

I walk her back to her room silently,
        her arm resting gently on mine.

Though firm of gait, she allows this comfort.
        My heart knows hers.

In every hello, she hears the echo of goodbye.

I hope you don't mind

A little girl recoils
at the white-bearded man
accepts a cupcake, wary hand
takes a delicate bite
Santa's eyes meet Mum's
      I hope you don't mind

A bank teller frowns
the boss asks, y'alright?
I'm really... not quite...
my sister just died
heart attack, fifty two
      I hope you don't mind

An old man stumbles
leans on a wall
afraid he might fall
just catchin' his breath
he'll be okay in a tic
      I hope you don't mind

Choking back tears
a woman returns toys
not for her 'Nana joys'
crumbled bank notes
poor exchange
      I hope you don't mind

An old woman sits
waiting a grown son
pondering battles won
adjusting to 'helpless'
eyes flitting around
      I hope you don't mind

An anxious young mother
rides the walkway
her boys halt in play
unaccustomed to Mum
worn out, overcome
      I hope you don't mind

A weary schoolboy
claims the middle of the road
backpack dragging, heavy load
moves but a little
to let cars pass
      I hope you don't mind

Geof and Graeme
your mum was tickled pink
well... that's what I think
I handed an icecream
leaving sticky fingers
      I hope you don't mind

gone

how long
will you
stay

if I only
have love
to offer?

oh,
you're already
gone.

indigo glass

It's a shame
you looked into the indigo glass
saw manipulation and greed
rejection and false love
ingenuine praise and vain need
bitterness and pride

It's a shame
you perceived a crystal ball
and not a mirror.

chasm

tectonic shift   how beautiful the ravage
each layer   a foundation of eons past
colours of earth   sienna umber ochre ecru
sliced in meticulous symmetry

deep blue   quivering waters beneath
breach the gap below
deceptive   deeper than ocean's millennia
cobalt serenity   connecting two worlds

inching apart   infinitesimal shift
unseen   unnoticed by city street throngs
continents adrift
ancient pervasive unstoppable

my weary heart   at the headland
swoops low in melancholy
unable to breach
the distance too great

silk

bound
by a silken plaited rope
that swings
searching
flailing
peeling layers from my soul

bound
by a wound
that cuts so deep
in brackish corners
misty edges
of my mind

bound
once by a cord
of blood and life
now torn
by villainy
and strife

bound
by a longing
that loops the stars
fuelled by a loving
that knows no wish
but this

your happiness

pedestal

I placed them on a pedestal
then I watched them fall
it was I who chose to put them there
not their fault at all.

Don't put me on a pedestal
I'm really not that tall
as surely as you place me there
that's the moment I will fall.

automaton

Hey there, Robot
fall into line
you're way off beam
and way out of line

You keep trying to think
you're something else
but you're just a robot
and nothing else

I've been trying to tell you
for many a year
and just when I finally
thought it was clear

You start you're thinking
and think you can feel
yet you still won't believe
your world isn't real

You're still not running to program
and you keep on repeating the same hum-drum
you've tried to tell me so many times before
that perhaps you march to a different drum

ode to spring

Spring
Oh, how I love thee...
Let me count the ways...

Time to burn the midnight oil
no cares for the heating bill
time to sort the garden
with more pizzazz than skill

Couldn't see much at 2 am
T'was better at break of light
not so good for falling over
when that last tree root gave up its fight

Off to Bunnings' confusing array
a test to DIY self confidence
gardening advice scarce from the staff
'Don't ask me, love. I kill succulents'

Sandpaper, rust kill, enamel, wall mounts
for the replacement loo roll kit
plaster board screws and a bottle of turps
off home to find the right drill bit

Winter boredom's a thing of the past
Dad tells a passing angel
'She falls down like her mother,
but she does a job that'll last'

There's no denying the Sun is brighter
muscles tighter, my purse is lighter
tools galore, a mess is in store
but what heck else is a kitchen for?

flickering embers

Flickering embers of my mind
melancholy shadows
flames gently dancing
soft warm glow
I can't let go

But how can I watch this grow
to a roaring fire
I can't control
to a reckless blaze
that sears my soul?

Flickering embers
as my heart remembers
I struggle to find
elusive answers
as the last flame shudders

Rekindle the ashes
quench not the flame
let me sit awhile
with these flickering embers
as my heart remembers
sweeter Decembers

Watagans

leaves scrunch underfoot
clear mountain air tantalises
pine cones huddle
memories scramble
for front row seats

in the forest
shadows add beauty

birdsong is phrased
by the echo of waterfalls
each a prelude to the next...

stone steps
rough hewn railing

sated we descent
the wishing well still waits
replete with my childhood coins

some people I know...

Sometimes
people don't understand
the things I do.

Like smacking a pick
into a cement slab
in my backyard at 1 am.

With only a thin layer
of cement over bricks
I soon had a nice pile of rubble.

The pick smacked down.
the bricks gave way
like warm butter

I toppled backwards
A precarious destination
My inevitable fate

Swift footwork
was needed
quick riverdance steps
the obvious answer
to add those precious inches
towards the soft lawn

Thump
I gazed at the night stars
lying there on my back
lush grass beneath me
and relief profound

'What the blazes are y'doing?'
asked the boarder
(He was social at 2 beers
Donald Trump at 4
Socrates at 6).

'Well,' says I
(aiming for rational)
'I don't want the bloke
who's comin tomorrow to quote
to con me with *'Madam,*
it's a difficult job'. When
for all I know I might've had
harder chocolates
to break apart.'

Now see
doesn't that make sense?
I knew you'd see it my way.

into the light

'It's not working,' I said.
'Keep trying,' He said.
'It's no good, I'm useless.'
Silence.

'It's not working. In the manual they say...'
'They don't know.'
'But *they* made the camera.'
'They didn't make your eyes.'
'So it is my fault.'
Silence.

'But I need...' I said.
Silence. I kicked a pebble.

'I'm grateful. I really need...'
Silence. I kicked a stone.

'I'm sorry, and I'm grateful. And I need...'
Silence. I kicked a rock.

'I give up. I don't even know how to ask.'
'It's not about asking,' He said.
'But how will you know...?'
'I am your Father.'
Silence—mine this time.

'Look the other way,' He said.
'What? But the camera...'
'It's not about the camera; it's about your eyes.'
'But everyone knows you have to take photos with the sun at your back!'
'If the sun is behind you, you are living in shadows.'

I turned; the shadows behind me now.
I looked; the brilliance of the sun glowed on every leaf.
I clicked the shutter.
Into the light.

'Oh!' I said. 'Thank you.'
'My pleasure.'
'So those things I need...?'

'I can't trust you yet; everything I give you, you give away.
Believe my gifts are for you.'
'Oh.' I wept a solitary tear of sadness. 'So it's not about needing or asking, gratitude or earning. It's about accepting.'
'Now you're listening.'

'Will you be silent again?'
'I was never silent.'
'Oh. It's not about hearing, it's about listening; knowing.'
'It's about the ears and eyes of the heart. I'll tell you more...'
'...when you can trust me,' I said.

I wept a solitary tear of understanding.
And looked.
Into the light.

'So I was never alone?'
'Not for a single heartbeat.'

I fought the Lord, and the Lord won

I looked within, and saw pain
I looked without and saw abandonment
I looked within and saw emptiness
I look up and saw nothing

life brought subtle changes
on the wings of peace
I looked in and saw joy
I looked up and saw heaven
through my mother's eyes
in that last goodbye

how fickle, how human
to make you in my image, God
to judge your presence
by the valleys in my life
to perceive your love
according to the tides
waxing and waning
reflecting my fortunes and fears

I saw no bridge home
would I ever find you again
what penance could I perform
what gift could I bring
you couldn't, wouldn't want me now
my knowledge of you
was built of human bricks
fired in the kiln of distorted frailty
seen through the mists
of false words and fears

I sat alone
were you in the heavens
upon a gold throne
waiting for me

to breach the distance?
how would I,
how could I?

all I could perceive
was a long and tortuous journey,
but before I even set out to find you
with my burdens and my losses,
before I thought to seek you
in cathedrals, pews and temples,
before I knew where you were
or how much I needed you

You found me

pity

I felt sorry for myself
sadness haunted me
mirrored back
from the sparkling glass windows
at the Westfield plaza

I saw a blind man
with my two good eyes
deftly waving his white cane
as he strode to some place or other
no pity indulged there

Hand thrust in my pocket
I saw a woman with one arm
carrying a water bottle with the stump
gaily chatting to a friend
no pity there either

An old man with a walking frame
slower than a boat without breeze
shuffled purposefully
with bright eyes, and rheumy hands
still no pity to be found

A television screen blinked at me
brown baked woman with glazed eyes
standing barefoot on orange sands
speaking of the ones left behind
taken, broken or maimed

I remembered being sorry for myself
I couldn't remember why.

gift

And so, myself I offer
all my loving heart can proffer
only the best will do

When I say the words
I want to live them

Words are only outward expressions
of inward impressions

So I can't risk losing you
with my heart accusing me
of giving only part of me
in place of
in regret of
the whole of me

So until then
I won't say the words
maybe
you've already read
between the lines

It's okay

It was a good relationship. If it seemed a bit one-sided I pushed it to the back of my mind. He was busy, important, powerful. I sang his praises. I imagined him singing mine. When I had doubts I faced them honestly with him, and then I felt better.

So what happened? Life happened. In all its ugly glory—past happiness was gone. Did he leave me? No, it was my father who crossed to his eternal peace, and I to eternal suffering.

I went outside, looked up at the black night sky and screamed, 'What the hell do you think you are doing?' Not a whisper came back on the frosty night air. He wasn't there - he'd left me too.

Gradually I began to talk to him again. First wary, then bolder; still my prayers were fierce.

Just when comfort began to grow, I fell further than I'd ever fallen before. Even my body betrayed me now. I clung to him; like a floundering ship in an endless storm. I prayed a lot - then.

I wrote prayers on the wall; too ill to rise. When the timeless years threw my weakened body up on the shore, there was no-one there. He had let me live - to live alone.

This time I sat quietly. I had some strength. As I looked down at my small son with his roaring voice, tangled mane and his alien fears, I realised I had much to do. I went outside, looked up at the cloudless sky and quietly said, 'It's okay if you're not there.'

I was still here, and would still do what I had to do for the same reasons I always did. I would love, I would nurture, and I would fight. I had no time to search for missing gods.

I fought many wars and won only one. For my son. I learned how to soothe his roaring voice; calm his tangled mane. Better still, when he was with me, he was no longer alien; no longer fearful.

My son grew stronger.
He learned to cope in the world when he was away from me, finding other places to belong, other worlds with soothing sounds. He discovered the magic of music - the joy of harmony. The beauty of 'other', and not just one.

One day he asked me, 'Why am I different? Will I be ok?'

We were sitting outside on a balmy day. I pointed to the tree in the backyard. 'Remember how you and your friends broke the tree's strongest branch?'

He bowed his head, his face awash with shame.

'Yes,' he answered quietly.

'Well, see it now?' I said, pointing to the tree, now lush and whole. 'See how one side has grown to balance the other and it looks just like it did before?'

'Yes!' His voice was brighter. 'How does it know to do that?'

'I don't know,' I said, 'it's mysterious and wonderful.'

I looked up at the blue, blue sky with its tiny whispers of clouds impatiently jostling each other.

'It's ok if you're there,' I whispered into the hesitant breeze and went inside, leaving the business of Being God to someone else.

For now, it was my purpose to be.

meet me here

I am mortal
you are divine
Meet me here.

I have failed in my search for you
Will you fail in your search for me?
I can't find you
find me
Meet me here.

Stretch out your finger
and cross the divide
that same journey you made so long ago
immortal to mortal
strength to weakness
God to man
Meet me here.

Silent witness to absence

they sit
with expectant sculpted pose
waiting
amid leaves of neglect
side by side
mute, complicit

Do I call her neighbour
when she's not there?
she resides in a care home
down the road
holding on to hope
she has a home, an address
and things

She's 93
I don't know her name
but I know my way home
by those solemn frogs
one day they'll be gone
like her

Voices woke me this morning
her family...
'It's a good day for it'
worry teases
I check her door
it's all still there
the frogs,
the plants Marg from No. 5 waters
the wandering leaves

I don't have to mourn
someone I've never met
not yet

unfaith-ful

She watches him with almond eyes. He stares
Unblinking, solid, frozen, wounded.
Measuring the space between them she advances
feet softly padding, sinuous curving of a feline.

For three days she wraps herself around his pain
willing him to forget her prowling indiscretion
her arched-back love-making against the rough tree.

Mewling soft sounds against his taut throat
have replaced screaming protestations.

Unfurling one long leg, she surrounds him
thigh against naked thigh. But
he's neutral, mind fug too dense to penetrate.

Her thin tattered camisole slips from a shoulder
firm rounded breasts caress bunching bicep
as she traces the dragon tattoo down his arm
gazing up through mascara-smudged eyes
her silken hair trapped in his five o'clock shadow
lush hair falling, shading tear stained lies.

She winds herself around him with timed perfection
his thumb rubs her palm, she purrs a sigh
retribution to forgiveness
not one word spoken.

She

She was the sort of friend who
on whom you relied, who said
'there, there' whenever you cried
although to be fair
it might've been
'go there, go further *to there*'

She was the sort of friend
who apologised after rifts
who said, 'I'm sorry *if*...
then opened the vault
on all your faults

She was the sort of friend
with time to visit all she knew
everyone that is, but you
a cheery hello through a crack
in the door—no breaking of bread,
please don't implore

She was the sort of friend
who finally finds time
'I'm all yours for a while'
then leaves with the gist
your every flaw for her mailing list

She was the sort of friend
with carefully phrased advice
nicely worded, neatly placed, totally nice
her real thoughts, that benevolent disdain
through kindness, with others,
your name to stain

The flies on your wall

The flies on your wall have been talking. You didn't see them, didn't notice their vibrations. Their silent flutterings. In the corners of the safe secret places of your walls. You don't think I know. It's not even that you've probed my broken pieces. Or that you decried my midnight angst. You think I deserve it deserve it all, chose it. And you're coming. To give voice to the words you've hidden, from me. You're packing, folding with precision, your clothes, your words. 'Sorry if ... things on my mind'. All precisely rehearsed as your itinerary. You don't think I know.

Void

We thought there was a bridge
spanning the space between. But
our connection to each other
we built on silences

On each side of the divide
we both strained our reach. But
across the mist and darkness
we built on silences

Halfway across the breach
with all the right intentions. But
we started out in different places
we built on silences

Guessing and assumptions
were grand and nobly sought. But
how could we meet across the chasm
we built on silences

And now as I am reaching
I'm hoping for your voice. But
you need to know I'm listening
nothing is built on silences

Teen wannabe queen

She would put an end to me now
if I were in her domain—her hive. But
she herself is not executioner, mistress
of my wax-celled exile. No,
not that. Not
yet

She presides
over worker-bees with their busy adoration. Over
drones with their willing subjugation. For
brief hope of conjugation. With their
quivering pollen legs. Their
noisy wings, their hum

Sole recipient of pheromones
she smoothly decides
who's in
and
who's out

Acutely attuned to sound
she hears coins clink, paper money crackle
a hundred yards away—Here
she comes for the pollen basket
dancing her slow dance
vibrating antennae
pupating young princess
seeking royal jell

The idea of you

I don't know if I mourn you
or the idea of you
        you are gone
my grief is tangible
I mourn a void, a definable loss
        but it's not an ache
for missed brunches, catchups
lost holidays
        or even absence
the thought that catches
and teases
sullen corners of my mind
        you didn't know me
I didn't know you
no matter how many
escarpments I climbed
I didn't find you
        who erected the barriers?
did I? did you?
        was it just a tragic farce?
of bad timing, myopic memory
or geography?

all I know—I sit alone
grieving a question
for the answer has scattered on the wind
        perhaps the same wind
that carried the ash
of your earthly unbeing
        and all that is left me—
to mourn
the idea of you

The portrait

With soft curding words he began.

With diligent focus and well-rehearsed phrases he parried.

With brutal gentility and second-hand brushes he jabbed at the canvas, the essence of her.

With cold eyes reproaching and broad strokes splashed boldly he created.

With loving indifference and solid irreverence he layered the colours.

With sharp convolutions and pressed intonations he thrust accusation, aiming to mortally wound.

With gaunt deprecation and bleak hand gestures he wove an image of who she must be.

With bland rhetoric staining, he framed each new summation.

With sated redress he released the malignant air that crowded his mind.

With dark-edged discipline from seasons unseen, he wrenched and thrust, his target assured.

With persistent inflection 'I'm not through yet', he waved aside her dim protestations.

With desperate ovation he sought yet to level the playing field of a game she knew not.

With crisp definition the brushstrokes revealed a portrait of himself.

With dawning clarity she perceived she had not known him, yet knew him better than he would ever know himself.

Tears cannot silent be

Goodbye
      my childhood hero
Live on
      sweet song of hope
God's breath
      is with you now
Soft and tender
      be the light
For your soul's
      heavenward flight

Today
      tears cannot silent be
      your struggling heart is free
Today
      you rest, safe at last
      earthly angst and pain is past
Today
      the aching void now ours to bear
      melding of sorrow the burden we share

Tomorrow
      when eternal day is dawning
      I'll see you on that other morning

without you

the world isn't the same without you

with your every look and sigh

those soft words of thanks

often stained with tears

or smiles of joy

you told me

my value

the world isn't the same without you

twice forever

Twice forever

If the moon should turn to stars

and fall like diamonds in the dust

if the sun should turn to moonbeams

and cast shadows of fiery rust

If the earth turns inside out

and March becomes December

I'll love you till twice forever

that's all you should remember

Kitchen table

At our last parting you gave me your stories and
I gave you mine. I gave you my kitchen table and
you gave me yours. I see
grooves and shadows where we often sat. Where
your family and friends had broken bread
all those years.

I hear shades of that laughter,
and those tears. There are scratches
on your table, and mine
grooved markings
of the written word, yours, theirs, maybe
even mine.

Friendship, the word itself
isn't sufficient
wide enough or wonderful enough
for the manner of loyalty and respect
you gave as instinctively as breathing. You put
your feet under my table.

You broke
bread at my table. And you stayed, stayed until
you declared my favourite chair
should be renamed as the 'bad back chair'. You
stayed. And anything else
isn't friendship.

God bless those who love enough
to break bread. Those who care sufficiently
to put their feet under our tables. Those
who sit and trace the grooves of life
and friendship.

What was I thinking?

God said,

'Gabriel, go down to earth. The human race is confounded, confused, lost and wandering. Since they forfeited face to face contact with me they've become worse. I don't know how else to say it. I thought they would get better. But no. I thought without my face shining so bright; without my face showing disappointment they would be happier; see things clearer. Like a blind man whose hearing improves when his sight has faded. *What was I thinking?*' Gabriel, I will try again. I will be clear, concise and end this confusion. I will give them my word through you. A message to them; right to their wondering hearts. But this time I will keep it simple. Gabriel, go down to earth and tell them this, this one thing, these three little words, 'Do unto others.'

Gabriel went down. He was gone a very long time. There seemed to be many more people actually there on earth than it appeared from heaven's lofty heights. It was hard to be in the midst of all that confusion. His head hurt. He got more tired that he did in heaven. When Gabriel returned, God said,

'What were you thinking?' God slapped Gabriel up the back of the head the way one would a recalcitrant schoolboy that one loves dearly but has caused frustration. 'I gave you three words. *Three words.* How did that become *one thousand* books, spawn *ten thousand* prophets who claim to have met me and *millions* of interpretations that are not even vaguely God-like? *What were you thinking?*'

Gabriel said,

'I know it looks bad. But I really did only give them just those three words. I was so pedantic about those three words that even when I ate with them I didn't ask them to pass the salt! I said no other words at all so they couldn't get it wrong. Every time anyone asked about you I said, 'Do unto others'. Those who met me quoted me and quoted you. Those who hadn't met me got jealous and said they had, and then quoted us both anyway, and pretty soon everyone thought they were quoting us when they were really quoting themselves. It was a nightmare. *You* made them that way. It's down to you, really.'

God said,

'What was I thinking? I got tired of robots. I thought that if I made beings capable of turning to me in freedom and love that they would face only one way; towards the light of my love. That they would find magnetic North. Find me. *What was I thinking?*'

Gabriel was touched by the humility of his master and said, 'Perhaps it *is* my fault. Perhaps I didn't hold my mouth right. Maybe my face betrayed the message. This is down to me.'

God was touched by the humility of his servant. And then he got an idea. God said,

'I will go down there. I will give them simple creeds. No rules. I will tell them stories. But mainly I will live among them. Just live.'

God went down himself. He was gone a very long time. There seemed to be many more people actually there on earth than it appeared from heaven's lofty heights. It was hard to be in the midst of all that confusion. His head hurt. He got more tired that he did in heaven. When he returned, God said,

'What was I thinking?'

The evening came. It was dinner time in heaven. It was God's favourite time of day. The whole family sitting down to discuss their day; to laugh, to sing, to tell stories. He looked at all those who had chosen Him. He turned to Gabriel.

'Gabriel...'

'I know,' said Gabriel, *'this* is what you were thinking.'

corner table

Winter's blast enters with me
slamming the glass door to the café
you're already here, pretending
not to wait, holding your gaunt frame erect

You move when you see me, stepping
forward with careful pace, waving
a pale tight-skinned hand, choosing
the table in a sunlit corner

You've aged twenty years in two, so thin
you almost fold in half. Wanting
information on the cancer, I lean in to hope
I didn't get the email attachment, I say

The left corner of your mouth jerks
the way it always has. You release
a deep sigh, then details: biopsies
mesothelioma, late stages, medications, prognosis

You accept the coffee, declining
the menu with minimal gesture, then
frown as I place gold coins on the table
I don't want ... anything, you say

We don't notice the ten am rush as
we measure our words
with resolute precision, stalling
and starting, clinging to script

You disappear into the street, drowning
in the traffic, leaving
me to walk the other way
I wish you'd let me say goodbye.

Author

L Linda Brooks lives in Adelaide. She has a BA Hons in Creative Writing. She gained a publisher for her childhood memoir 'A Curious & Inelegant Childhood'. She has written two books on Asperger's Syndrome with Professor Tony Attwood: 'I'm not broken, I'm just different' and 'Callan the Chameleon'. Published in anthologies: 'Coastlines' 5, 6, 7 & 8; 'Wood, Bricks & Stone'; 'Grieve' and 'Longing for Solitude'. Awards: Rebecca Coyle Scholarship for Hons; first prize for The Legacy University Level Creative Writing Award; first prize in the Gabe Reynaud Creative Writing Award and the Mater Misericordiae Grieve Writing Award.

Linda's characters have resilience and warmth and her books are enriched by wit, spirit and surprise. She attributes this mix to her Irish/British convict heritage. Sharp observation is crafted with depth and compassion, as she explores the human experience with fearless candour. Many of Linda's books feature her skill as an artist and illustrator.

Other titles by Linda

Nonfiction:
An Australian Childhood

Poetry:
Seeking the Sun Central Coast Poetry
Third Wednesday Poets – an anthology

Adult fiction:
Behind Whispering Hands
The Unprize
A broken hallelujah
Under the Bracken Fern
Scarlett doesn't live here anymore

Children's books:
A Tabby Never Forgets
Beth's Christmas Wish
Callan the Chameleon (Asperger's Syndrome)
Dusty Bunny's Very Important Job
Ethereal Land
Izzy & Pudding the Cat
I want a monkey!
Madam Iris Bigglesworth
The Frog that Hiccupped
When the stars move
Who Stole Christmas?

Publisher of the anthologies:
We are Australian
The Great Australian Shed
Waltzing Matilda